Publications International, Ltd.
Favorite Brand Name Recipes at www.fbnr.com

Louis Weber, CEO
Publications International, Ltd.
7373 North Cicero Avenue
Lincolnwood, Illinois 60712

Recipe Development: The Lipton Kitchens
Brand Manager: AnneMarie Cesario
Home Economist/Project Coordinator: Lauren Dellabella
Test Kitchen Assistant: Liliana Mendoza
Project Administrator: Michelle Febres

Photography: Sacco Studio Chicago, IL
Photographer: Tom O'Connell
Prop Stylist: Chris Jakab
Food Stylists: Kim Hartman and Diane Hugh
Assistant Food Stylist: Liza Brown, R.D.

Pictured on the front cover: Roasted Chicken au Jus *(page 72).*

Pictured on the back cover *(clockwise from top left):* The Famous Lipton California Dip *(page 8),* Onion-Roasted Potatoes *(page 20)* and Lipton Onion Burgers *(page 36).*

ISBN: 0-7853-3891-8

Manufactured in China.

8 7 6 5 4 3 2 1

Lipton®
RECIPE SECRETS®
RECIPE SOUP MIX
The Magic of Flavor™

Do You Believe in the Magic of Flavor?

Wouldn't it be great to have a cookbook of culinary "magic" at your fingertips whenever you need to easily transform your everyday foods into irresistible dishes? A cookbook that contains mouthwatering, foolproof recipes you can always count on to perk up a party or excite any get-together? Well, we believe in magic—the magic that happens when **Lipton® Recipe Secrets® Soup Mix** transforms the flavor of your chicken, potato and beef dishes into so much more!

Our new Garlic Mushroom Soup Mix, with its blend of sautéed garlic and tender mushroom pieces, is the perfect partner for sensational chicken dishes like

p. 54

Crispy Garlic Chicken and Roasted Chicken au Jus. Of course, our Onion Soup Mix continues to work its magic on tempting Onion-Roasted Potatoes, yummy Pizza Meat Loaf and the ever-popular Lipton Onion Burgers. Dazzle them with a dip. Let Lipton Recipe Secrets do it right with appetizing offerings such as Lipton Roasted Red Pepper & Onion Dip and Creamy Garlic Salsa Dip. When you cook with our Lipton Recipe Secrets Soup Mix, it's more than just ordinary food—it's truly an extraordinary experience!

Filled with 71 simple, yet delicious, recipes guaranteed to turn ordinary foods into irresistible favorites, this cookbook makes it easy to find the perfect recipe for every occasion. Whip up one of our great, easy-fix dips whenever you're in the mood for something wonderful. Don't settle for ho-hum side dishes—ours will take center stage on your plate thanks to the magic touch of Lipton Recipe Secrets. Fire up the grill and get sizzlin' with our tempting burgers, chicken and grilled salads! For casual weekday get-togethers, you'll enjoy our homey favorites that sooth and satisfy at the end of a busy workday. And to get the weekend in full swing, create savory specialties that are guaranteed to please everyone.

Get started—open this cookbook and enjoy a whole new world of cooking with style and confidence. Now that's magic in the making!

For simple and delicious recipes and ideas, visit us on the web at **www.recipesecrets.com.**

Great Dipping Ideas

The Famous Lipton California Dip

1 envelope Lipton Recipe Secrets Onion Soup Mix
1 container (16 ounces) regular or light sour cream

1. In medium bowl, combine all ingredients; chill at least 2 hours.

2. Serve with your favorite dippers. *Makes 2 cups dip*

Note: For a creamier dip, add more sour cream.

The Famous Lipton California Dip

Hot Garlic Artichoke Dip

1 envelope Lipton Recipe Secrets Garlic Mushroom Soup Mix
1 can (14 ounces) artichoke hearts, drained and chopped
1 cup mayonnaise
1 container (8 ounces) sour cream
1 cup shredded Swiss or mozzarella cheese (about 4 ounces)

1. Preheat oven to 350°F. In 1-quart casserole, combine all ingredients.

2. Bake uncovered 30 minutes or until heated through.

3. Serve with your favorite dippers. *Makes 3 cups dip*

Variation: For a cold artichoke dip, omit Swiss cheese. Stir in, if desired, ¼ cup grated Parmesan cheese. Do not bake.

◆ Also terrific with Lipton Recipe Secrets Savory Herb with Garlic or Onion Soup Mix.

Recipe Tip

For a quick party fix or anytime treat, try these CLASSIC LIPTON DIPS: Combine 1 envelope Lipton Recipe Secrets Onion, Garlic Mushroom, Savory Herb with Garlic, Onion-Mushroom, Beefy Onion, Beefy Mushroom, Golden Onion, Vegetable or Fiesta Herb with Red Pepper Soup Mix with 1 container (16 ounces) sour cream. Chill and serve with your favorite dippers.

Hot Garlic Artichoke Dip

Lipton Roasted Red Pepper & Onion Dip

1 envelope Lipton Recipe Secrets Onion Soup Mix
1 container (16 ounces) regular or light sour cream
1 jar (7 ounces) roasted red peppers, drained and chopped

1. In small bowl, combine all ingredients; chill at least 2 hours.

2. Serve with your favorite dippers. *Makes 2 cups dip*

◆ Also terrific with Lipton Recipe Secrets Garlic Mushroom or Savory Herb with Garlic Soup Mix.

White Pizza Dip

1 envelope Lipton Recipe Secrets Savory Herb with Garlic Soup Mix
1 container (16 ounces) sour cream
1 cup ricotta cheese
1 cup shredded mozzarella cheese (about 4 ounces)
¼ cup chopped pepperoni (about 1 ounce) (optional)

1. Preheat oven to 350°F. In 1-quart casserole, combine soup mix, sour cream, ricotta cheese, ¾ cup mozzarella cheese and pepperoni. Sprinkle with remaining ¼ cup mozzarella cheese.

2. Bake uncovered 30 minutes or until heated through.

3. Serve, if desired, with sliced Italian or French bread.

Makes 2 cups dip

◆ Also terrific with Lipton Recipe Secrets Garlic Mushroom or Fiesta Herb with Red Pepper Soup Mix.

Lipton Roasted Red Pepper & Onion Dip

Extra Special Spinach Dip

1 envelope Lipton Recipe Secrets Vegetable Soup Mix
1 container (8 ounces) regular or light sour cream
1 cup regular or light mayonnaise
1 package (10 ounces) frozen chopped spinach, thawed and squeezed dry
1 can (8 ounces) water chestnuts, drained and chopped (optional)

1. In medium bowl, combine all ingredients; chill at least 2 hours.

2. Serve with your favorite dippers. *Makes 3 cups dip*

◆ Also terrific with Lipton Recipe Secrets Garlic Mushroom, Savory Herb with Garlic or Fiesta Herb with Red Pepper Soup Mix.

Springtime California Dip

1 envelope Lipton Recipe Secrets Onion Soup Mix
1 container (16 ounces) sour cream
1 large tomato, chopped
1 cup peeled, seeded and chopped cucumber

1. In medium bowl, combine all ingredients; chill at least 2 hours.

2. Serve with your favorite dippers. *Makes 4 cups dip*

Extra Special Spinach Dip

Hot French Onion Dip

1 envelope Lipton Recipe Secrets Onion Soup Mix
1 container (16 ounces) sour cream
2 cups shredded Swiss cheese (about 8 ounces)
¼ cup mayonnaise

1. Preheat oven to 375°F. In 1-quart casserole, combine soup mix, sour cream, 1¾ cups Swiss cheese and mayonnaise.

2. Bake uncovered 20 minutes or until heated through. Sprinkle with remaining ¼ cup cheese.

3. Serve, if desired, with sliced French bread or your favorite dippers.

Makes 2 cups dip

Warm Broccoli 'n Cheddar Dip

1 envelope Lipton Recipe Secrets Garlic Mushroom Soup Mix
1 container (16 ounces) sour cream
1 package (10 ounces) frozen chopped broccoli or spinach, thawed and squeezed dry
1 cup shredded Cheddar cheese (about 4 ounces)

1. Preheat oven to 350°F. In 1-quart casserole, combine soup mix, sour cream, broccoli and ¾ cup cheese. Sprinkle with remaining ¼ cup cheese.

2. Bake uncovered 30 minutes or until heated through.

3. Serve with your favorite dippers.

Makes 3 cups dip

◆ Also terrific with Lipton Recipe Secrets Savory Herb with Garlic, Vegetable or Golden Onion Soup Mix.

Hot French Onion Dip

Creamy Garlic Salsa Dip

1 envelope Lipton Recipe Secrets Garlic Mushroom Soup Mix
1 container (16 ounces) sour cream
½ cup your favorite salsa

1. In medium bowl, combine all ingredients; chill at least 2 hours.

2. Serve with your favorite dippers. *Makes 2½ cups dip*

◆ Also terrific with Lipton Recipe Secrets Onion or Savory Herb with Garlic Soup Mix.

Warm Vegetable & Seafood Dip

1 envelope Lipton Recipe Secrets Vegetable Soup Mix
1 container (16 ounces) sour cream
1 can (6½ ounces) imitation crabmeat, cooked shrimp or 1 cup frozen cooked crabmeat, thawed
3 ounces cream cheese, softened
1 teaspoon lemon juice

1. Preheat oven to 325°F. In 1-quart casserole, combine all ingredients.

2. Bake uncovered 30 minutes or until heated through.

3. Serve with your favorite dippers. *Makes 3 cups dip*

◆ Also terrific with Lipton Recipe Secrets Garlic Mushroom, Savory Herb with Garlic or Fiesta Herb with Red Pepper Soup Mix.

Creamy Garlic Salsa Dip

On the Side

Onion-Roasted Potatoes

1 envelope Lipton Recipe Secrets Onion Soup Mix
4 medium all-purpose potatoes, cut into large chunks (about 2 pounds)
⅓ cup olive or vegetable oil

1. Preheat oven to 450°F. In large plastic bag or bowl, add all ingredients. Close bag and shake, or toss in bowl, until potatoes are evenly coated.

2. In 13×9-inch baking or roasting pan, arrange potatoes; discard bag.

3. Bake uncovered, stirring occasionally, 40 minutes or until potatoes are tender and golden brown. *Makes 4 servings*

◆ Also terrific with Lipton Recipe Secrets Garlic Mushroom, Onion-Mushroom, Golden Onion, Savory Herb with Garlic or Fiesta Herb with Pepper Soup Mix.

Onion-Roasted Potatoes

Lipton Recipe Secrets Recipe Soup Mix

Broccoli Casserole with Crumb Topping

2 slices day-old white bread, coarsely crumbled (about 1¼ cups)
½ cup shredded mozzarella cheese (about 2 ounces)
2 tablespoons chopped fresh parsley (optional)
2 tablespoons olive or vegetable oil
1 clove garlic, finely chopped
6 cups broccoli florets and/or cauliflowerets
1 envelope Lipton Recipe Secrets Onion Soup Mix
1 cup water
1 large tomato, chopped

1. In small bowl, combine bread crumbs, cheese, parsley, 1 tablespoon oil and garlic; set aside.

2. In 12-inch skillet, heat remaining 1 tablespoon oil over medium heat and cook broccoli, stirring frequently, 2 minutes.

3. Stir in soup mix blended with water. Bring to a boil over high heat. Reduce heat to low and simmer uncovered, stirring occasionally, 8 minutes or until broccoli is almost tender. Add tomato and simmer 2 minutes.

4. Spoon vegetable mixture into 1½-quart casserole; top with bread crumb mixture. Broil 1½ minutes or until crumbs are golden and cheese is melted.

Makes 6 servings

◆ Also terrific with Lipton Recipe Secrets Garlic Mushroom Soup Mix.

Broccoli Casserole with Crumb Topping

Garlic Mashed Potatoes

6 medium all-purpose potatoes, peeled, if desired, and cut into chunks (about 3 pounds)
Water
1 envelope Lipton Recipe Secrets Garlic Mushroom Soup Mix
½ cup milk
½ cup margarine or butter, softened

1. In 4-quart saucepan, cover potatoes with water; bring to a boil.

2. Reduce heat to low and simmer uncovered 20 minutes or until potatoes are very tender; drain.

3. Return potatoes to saucepan, then mash. Stir in remaining ingredients.

Makes 8 servings

◆ Also terrific with Lipton Recipe Secrets Savory Herb with Garlic, Onion or Golden Onion Soup Mix.

Lipton Onion Gravy

1 envelope Lipton Recipe Secrets Onion Soup Mix
2 tablespoons all-purpose flour
2 cups water

1. In medium saucepan, combine soup mix and flour; stir in water.

2. Bring to a boil over high heat, stirring occasionally. Reduce heat to medium and simmer uncovered, stirring occasionally, 5 minutes or until gravy is thickened.

Makes 1¾ cups gravy

◆ Also terrific with Lipton Recipe Secrets Garlic Mushroom, Golden Onion, Beefy Onion or Beefy Mushroom Soup Mix.

Garlic Mashed Potatoes

Mashed Onion-Roasted Potatoes

1 envelope Lipton Recipe Secrets Onion Soup Mix
4 medium all-purpose potatoes, cut into large chunks (about 2 pounds)
⅓ cup olive or vegetable oil
1¾ cups hot milk

1. Preheat oven to 450°F. In large plastic bag or bowl, add all ingredients except milk. Close bag and shake, or toss in bowl, until potatoes are evenly coated.

2. In 13×9-inch baking or roasting pan, arrange potatoes; discard bag.

3. Bake uncovered, stirring occasionally, 40 minutes or until potatoes are tender and golden brown.

4. Turn potatoes into large bowl. Mash potatoes; stir in hot milk.

Makes 4 servings

◆ Also terrific with Lipton Recipe Secrets Garlic Mushroom or Savory Herb with Garlic Soup Mix.

Recipe Tip

To peel or not to peel, that is the question. When making mashed potatoes, leave the skins on for extra nutrient retention and wonderful flavor. Best of all, you'll spend less time in the kitchen.

Garlic Fries

1 envelope Lipton Recipe Secrets Savory Herb with Garlic Soup Mix
1 cup plain dry bread crumbs
2 pounds large red or all-purpose potatoes, cut lengthwise into wedges
⅓ cup margarine or butter, melted

1. Preheat oven to 400°F. In large bowl, blend soup mix with bread crumbs. Dip potatoes in margarine, then soup mixture, until evenly coated.

2. In 15½×10½×1-inch jelly-roll pan sprayed with nonstick cooking spray, arrange potatoes in single layer.

3. Bake uncovered 40 minutes or until potatoes are tender and golden brown.

Makes 4 servings

◆ Also terrific with Lipton Recipe Secrets Garlic Mushroom, Onion or Fiesta Herb with Red Pepper Soup Mix.

Roasted Idaho & Sweet Potatoes

1 envelope Lipton Recipe Secrets Onion Soup Mix
2 medium all-purpose potatoes, peeled, if desired, and cut into large chunks (about 1 pound)
2 medium sweet potatoes or yams, peeled, if desired, and cut into large chunks (about 1 pound)
¼ cup olive or vegetable oil

1. Preheat oven to 425°F. In large plastic bag or bowl, add all ingredients. Close bag and shake, or toss in bowl, until potatoes are evenly coated.

2. In 13×9-inch baking or roasting pan, arrange potatoes; discard bag.

3. Bake uncovered, stirring occasionally, 40 minutes or until potatoes are tender and golden. *Makes 4 servings*

Skillet Green Beans

2 tablespoons margarine or butter
1 medium onion, cut into thin wedges
1 large tomato, diced
1 pound green beans, trimmed
1 envelope Lipton Recipe Secrets Garlic Mushroom Soup Mix
¾ cup water

1. In 12-inch skillet, melt margarine over medium heat and cook onion, stirring occasionally, 5 minutes or until tender.

2. Stir in tomato and green beans and cook over medium-high heat 5 minutes. Stir in soup mix blended with water.

3. Simmer covered 10 minutes or until green beans are tender.
Makes 4 servings

Roasted Idaho & Sweet Potatoes

Vegetable Parmesan Bake

- **1 envelope Lipton Recipe Secrets Garlic Mushroom Soup Mix**
- **¼ cup grated Parmesan cheese**
- **1 large baking potato, cut into ¼-inch-thick slices**
- **1 medium zucchini, diagonally cut into ¼-inch-thick slices**
- **1 large tomato, cut into ¼-inch-thick slices**
- **1 tablespoon margarine or butter, cut into small pieces**

1. Preheat oven to 375°F. In small bowl, combine soup mix and Parmesan cheese; set aside.

2. In shallow 1-quart casserole sprayed with nonstick cooking spray, arrange potato slices, overlapping slightly. Sprinkle with ⅓ of the soup mixture. Top with zucchini slices, overlapping slightly. Sprinkle with ⅓ of the soup mixture. Top with tomato slices, overlapping slightly. Sprinkle with remaining soup mixture. Top with margarine.

3. Bake covered 40 minutes. Remove cover and bake an additional 10 minutes or until vegetables are tender.

Makes 4 servings

Recipe Tip

For delicious tomatoes any time of the year, store them on your kitchen counter out of direct sunlight as sunlight can change their color without ripening the flavor or texture. And never store them in the refrigerator as this can spoil their flavor and texture.

Vegetable Parmesan Bake

Oven-Roasted Vegetables

1 envelope Lipton Recipe Secrets Savory Herb with Garlic Soup Mix
1½ pounds assorted fresh vegetables*
2 tablespoons olive or vegetable oil

1. Preheat oven to 450°F. In large plastic bag or bowl, add all ingredients. Close bag and shake, or toss in bowl, until vegetables are evenly coated.

2. In 13×9-inch baking or roasting pan, arrange vegetables; discard bag.

3. Bake uncovered, stirring once, 20 minutes or until vegetables are tender.

Makes 4 servings

*Use any combination of the following, sliced: zucchini, yellow squash, red, green or yellow bell peppers, carrots, celery and mushrooms.

Tip: For a lower fat version, spray pan lightly with nonstick cooking spray and replace oil with 2 tablespoons water.

◆ Also terrific with Lipton Recipe Secrets Garlic Mushroom, Onion or Golden Onion Soup Mix.

Garlic Mushroom Rice

2½ cups water
1 envelope Lipton Recipe Secrets Garlic Mushroom Soup Mix
1 cup uncooked regular or converted rice

1. In 2-quart saucepan, bring water to a boil over high heat. Stir in soup mix and rice.

2. Reduce heat and simmer covered 20 minutes. *Makes 3 servings*

Note: Also terrific with Lipton Recipe Secrets Golden Onion, Onion-Mushroom, Savory Herb with Garlic or Onion Soup Mix.

Savory Roasted Potatoes

1 envelope Lipton Recipe Secrets Onion Soup Mix
4 medium all-purpose potatoes, cut into large chunks (about 2 pounds)
⅓ cup margarine or butter, melted
1 teaspoon garlic powder
1 teaspoon soy sauce

1. Preheat oven to 450°F. In large plastic bag or bowl, add all ingredients. Close bag and shake, or toss in bowl, until potatoes are evenly coated.

2. In 13×9-inch baking or roasting pan, arrange potatoes; discard bag.

3. Bake uncovered, stirring occasionally, 40 minutes or until potatoes are tender and golden brown. *Makes 4 servings*

Recipe Tip

Always use the correct pan size for perfectly roasted dishes. The pan should be large enough to hold the food comfortably to allow for browning and caramelization. Avoid a pan that's too small as the food will be overcrowded and won't brown properly.

Scalloped Garlic Potatoes

3 medium all-purpose potatoes, peeled and thinly sliced (about 1½ pounds)
1 envelope Lipton Recipe Secrets Garlic Mushroom Soup Mix
1 cup (½ pint) whipping or heavy cream
½ cup water

1. Preheat oven to 375°F. In lightly greased 2-quart shallow baking dish, arrange potatoes. In medium bowl, blend remaining ingredients; pour over potatoes.

2. Bake uncovered 45 minutes or until potatoes are tender.

Makes 4 servings

◆ Also terrific with Lipton Recipe Secrets Savory Herb with Garlic Soup Mix.

Buffalo Potatoes

1 envelope Lipton Recipe Secrets Savory Herb with Garlic Soup Mix
⅓ cup margarine or butter, melted
1 to 2 tablespoons hot pepper sauce
4 medium baking potatoes, cut lengthwise into wedges (about 2 pounds)
Wish-Bone® Chunky Blue Cheese Dressing

1. Preheat oven to 450°F. In large plastic bag or bowl, add all ingredients except Wish-Bone Dressing. Close bag and shake, or toss in bowl, until potatoes are evenly coated.

2. In 13×9-inch baking or roasting pan, arrange potatoes; discard bag.

3. Bake uncovered, stirring occasionally, 45 minutes or until potatoes are crisp. Serve with Wish-Bone Dressing. *Makes 4 servings*

◆ Also terrific with Lipton Recipe Secrets Onion Soup Mix.

Scalloped Garlic Potatoes

Hot off the Grill

Lipton Onion Burgers

1 envelope Lipton Recipe Secrets Onion Soup Mix
2 pounds ground beef
½ cup water

1. In large bowl, combine all ingredients; shape into 8 patties.

2. Grill or broil until done. Serve, if desired, on hamburger buns.

Makes 8 servings

◆ Also terrific with Lipton Recipe Secrets Garlic Mushroom, Beefy Onion, Onion-Mushroom, Beefy Mushroom, Savory Herb with Garlic or Fiesta Herb with Red Pepper Soup Mix.

Lipton Onion Burger

Garlic Rubbed Chicken

1 envelope Lipton Recipe Secrets Garlic Mushroom Soup Mix
3 tablespoons olive or vegetable oil
6 boneless, skinless chicken breast halves (about 1¾ pounds)

1. In small bowl, combine soup mix and oil; rub mixture on chicken.

2. Grill or broil until chicken is no longer pink. *Makes 4 servings*

◆ Also terrific with Lipton Recipe Secrets Savory Herb with Garlic Soup Mix.

Recipe Tip

For a SWEET 'N SPICY ONION GLAZE, combine 1 envelope Lipton Recipe Secrets Onion Soup Mix, 1 jar (20 ounces) apricot preserves and 1 cup Wish-Bone® Sweet 'n Spicy French or Russian Dressing. Remove the amount of glaze needed for chicken, spareribs, kabobs, hamburgers or frankfurters. Brush glaze on during the last half of grilling, broiling or baking. Store the remaining glaze covered in the refrigerator for up to 2 weeks. Makes about 2½ cups glaze.

Garlic Rubbed Chicken

Lipton RECIPE SECRETS RECIPE SOUP MIX

Golden Glazed Flank Steak

- 1 envelope Lipton Recipe Secrets Onion Soup Mix
- 1 jar (12 ounces) apricot or peach preserves
- ½ cup water
- 1 beef flank steak (about 2 pounds), cut into thin strips
- 2 medium green, red and/or yellow bell peppers, sliced
- Hot cooked rice

1. In small bowl, combine soup mix, preserves and water; set aside.

2. On heavy-duty aluminum foil or in bottom of broiler pan with rack removed, arrange steak and peppers; top with soup mixture.

3. Grill or broil, turning steak and vegetables once, until steak is done. Serve over hot rice.

Makes 8 servings

◆ Also terrific with Lipton Recipe Secrets Onion-Mushroom, Garlic Mushroom or Fiesta Herb with Red Pepper Soup Mix.

Recipe Tip

Dried herbs and spices should be replaced every 6 to 9 months before they lose their flavor. Instead of simply throwing them away, throw a handful of old herbs on your coals when grilling for added flavor.

Grilled Vegetable Sandwiches

2 pounds assorted fresh vegetables*
1 envelope Lipton Recipe Secrets Garlic Mushroom Soup Mix
⅓ cup olive or vegetable oil
2 tablespoons balsamic or red wine vinegar
½ teaspoon dried basil leaves, crushed
4 (8-inch) pita breads, warmed
4 ounces crumbled Montrachet, shredded mozzarella, Jarlsberg, Monterey Jack or Cheddar cheese

1. In large bowl, combine vegetables and soup mix blended with oil, vinegar and basil until evenly coated.

2. Grill or broil vegetables until tender. To serve, cut 1-inch strip off each pita. Fill with vegetables and sprinkle with cheese. Garnish, if desired, with shredded lettuce and sliced tomato. *Makes 4 servings*

*Use any combination of the following, sliced: red, green or yellow bell peppers, mushrooms, zucchini or eggplant.

◆ Also terrific with Lipton Recipe Secrets Onion, Savory Herb with Garlic, Fiesta Herb with Red Pepper or Golden Onion Soup Mix.

Cheesy Spinach Burgers

- **1 envelope Lipton Recipe Secrets Garlic Mushroom Soup Mix**
- **2 pounds ground beef**
- **1 package (10 ounces) frozen chopped spinach, thawed and squeezed dry**
- **1 cup shredded mozzarella or Cheddar cheese (about 4 ounces)**

1. In large bowl, combine all ingredients; shape into 8 patties.

2. Grill or broil until done. Serve, if desired, on hamburger buns.

Makes 8 servings

◆ Also terrific with Lipton Recipe Secrets Onion Soup Mix.

Recipe Tip

LIPTON ONION BUTTER makes a terrific topping for vegetables, potatoes, hot bread or rolls. Thoroughly blend 1 envelope Lipton Recipe Secrets Onion Soup Mix with ¾ cup softened butter or margarine. Store covered in the refrigerator. Makes 1 cup.

Cheesy Spinach Burger

Grilled Potato Salad

1 envelope Lipton Recipe Secrets Onion Soup Mix
⅓ cup olive or vegetable oil
2 tablespoons red wine vinegar
1 clove garlic, finely chopped
2 pounds small red or all-purpose potatoes, cut into 1-inch cubes
1 tablespoon fresh basil, chopped or 1 teaspoon dried basil leaves, crushed
Freshly ground black pepper

1. In large bowl, blend soup mix, oil, vinegar and garlic; stir in potatoes.

2. Grease 30×18-inch sheet of heavy-duty aluminum foil; top with potato mixture. Wrap foil loosely around mixture, sealing edges airtight with double fold. Place on another sheet of 30×18-inch foil; seal edges airtight with double fold in opposite direction.

3. Grill, shaking package occasionally and turning package once, 40 minutes or until potatoes are tender. Spoon into serving bowl and toss with basil and pepper. Serve slightly warm or at room temperature. *Makes 4 servings*

Oven Method: Preheat oven to 450°F. Prepare foil packet as above. Place in large baking pan on bottom rack and bake, turning packet once, 40 minutes or until potatoes are tender. Toss and serve as above.

◆ Also terrific with Lipton Recipe Secrets Onion-Mushroom or Golden Onion Soup Mix.

Grilled Potato Salad

Fresco Marinated Chicken

1 envelope Lipton Recipe Secrets Garlic Mushroom Soup Mix
⅓ cup water
¼ cup olive or vegetable oil
1 teaspoon lemon juice or vinegar
4 boneless, skinless chicken breast halves (about 1¼ pounds)

1. For marinade, blend all ingredients except chicken.

2. In shallow baking dish or plastic bag, pour ½ cup of the marinade over chicken. Cover, or close bag, and marinate in refrigerator, turning occasionally, up to 3 hours. Refrigerate remaining marinade.

3. Remove chicken, discarding marinade. Grill or broil chicken, turning once and brushing with refrigerated marinade until chicken is no longer pink.

Makes 4 servings

◆ Also terrific with Lipton Recipe Secrets Savory Herb with Garlic or Golden Onion Soup Mix.

Garden Garlic Burgers

1½ pounds ground beef or turkey
1 envelope Lipton Recipe Secrets Garlic Mushroom Soup Mix
2 small carrots, finely shredded
1 small zucchini, shredded
1 egg, slightly beaten
¼ cup plain dry bread crumbs

1. In large bowl, combine all ingredients; shape into 6 patties.

2. Grill or broil until done. Serve, if desired, on hamburger buns or whole wheat rolls.

Makes 6 servings

◆ Also terrific with Lipton Recipe Secrets Onion, Savory Herb with Garlic or Onion-Mushroom Soup Mix.

Tempting Taco Burgers

1 envelope Lipton Recipe Secrets Onion-Mushroom Soup Mix
1 pound ground beef
½ cup chopped tomato
¼ cup finely chopped green bell pepper
1 teaspoon chili powder
¼ cup water

1. In large bowl, combine all ingredients; shape into 4 patties.

2. Grill or broil until done. Serve, if desired, on hamburger buns and top with shredded lettuce and Cheddar cheese. *Makes 4 servings*

◆ Also terrific with Lipton Recipe Secrets Onion, Garlic Mushroom, Beefy Onion or Beefy Mushroom Soup Mix.

Recipe Tip

The best way to test for doneness of beef, pork, fish and poultry is to use a meat thermometer or an instant read thermometer. But, you may want to try this quick touch test first: Gently press a piece of uncooked flesh to feel what rare feels like; the flesh will become tighter and more resistant as it cooks. Medium will have some give; well-done will be quite firm.

Souper Stuffed Cheese Burgers

1 envelope Lipton Recipe Secrets Onion Soup Mix
2 pounds ground beef
½ cup water
¾ cup shredded Cheddar, mozzarella or Monterey Jack cheese (about 6 ounces)

1. In large bowl, combine soup mix, ground beef and water; shape into 12 patties.

2. Place 2 tablespoons cheese in center of 6 patties. Top with remaining patties and seal edges tightly.

3. Grill or broil until done. Serve, if desired, on onion poppy seed rolls.

Makes 6 servings

◆ Also terrific with Lipton Recipe Secrets Garlic Mushroom, Savory Herb with Garlic, Onion-Mushroom or Beefy Onion Soup Mix.

Recipe Tip

To perk up your burgers, serve them on something besides a bun. Try bagels, English muffins, pita bread or even tortillas for a fun change of pace!

Souper Stuffed Cheese Burger and Garlic Fries (page 27)

Honey-Lime Pork Chops

1 envelope Lipton Recipe Secrets Savory Herb with Garlic Soup Mix
⅓ cup soy sauce
3 tablespoons honey
3 tablespoons lime juice
1 teaspoon grated fresh ginger or ¼ teaspoon ground ginger (optional)
4 pork chops, 1½ inches thick

1. For marinade, blend all ingredients except pork chops.

2. In shallow baking dish or plastic bag, pour ½ cup of the marinade over chops; turn to coat. Cover, or close bag, and marinate in refrigerator, turning occasionally, 2 to 24 hours. Refrigerate remaining marinade.

3. Remove chops from marinade, discarding marinade. Grill or broil chops, turning once and brushing with refrigerated marinade, until chops are done.

Makes 4 servings

◆ Also terrific with Lipton Recipe Secrets Garlic Mushroom or Onion Soup Mix.

Grilled Reuben Burgers

1 envelope Lipton Recipe Secrets Onion-Mushroom Soup Mix
½ cup water
1½ pounds ground beef
½ cup shredded Swiss cheese (about 2 ounces)
1 tablespoon crisp-cooked crumbled bacon or bacon bits
½ teaspoon caraway seeds (optional)

1. In large bowl, combine all ingredients; shape into 6 patties.

2. Grill or broil until done. Top, if desired, with heated sauerkraut and additional bacon. *Makes 6 servings*

◆ Also terrific with Lipton Recipe Secrets Onion or Beefy Onion Soup Mix.

Grilled Pasta Salad

4 medium zucchini and/or yellow squash, sliced
1 medium Spanish onion, cut into large chunks
1 envelope Lipton Recipe Secrets Garlic Mushroom Soup Mix
¼ cup olive or vegetable oil
8 ounces penne, rotini or ziti pasta, cooked and drained
¾ cup chopped roasted red peppers
2 tablespoons balsamic vinegar (optional)

1. On heavy-duty aluminum foil or broiler pan, arrange zucchini and onion. Brush with soup mix blended with oil.

2. Grill or broil 5 minutes or until golden brown and crisp-tender.

3. In large bowl, toss cooked pasta, vegetables, roasted peppers and vinegar. Serve warm or at room temperature. *Makes 4 main-dish or 8 side-dish servings*

◆ Also terrific with Lipton Recipe Secrets Savory Herb with Garlic or Golden Onion Soup Mix.

Weekday Get-togethers

Crispy Garlic Chicken

1 envelope Lipton Recipe Secrets Garlic Mushroom Soup Mix
⅓ cup mayonnaise
¼ cup grated Parmesan cheese
4 boneless, skinless chicken breast halves (about 1¼ pounds)
2 tablespoons plain dry bread crumbs

1. Preheat oven to 400°F. In medium bowl, combine soup mix, mayonnaise and cheese; set aside.

2. On baking sheet, arrange chicken. Evenly top chicken with soup mixture, then evenly sprinkle with bread crumbs.

3. Bake uncovered 20 minutes or until chicken is no longer pink.

Makes 4 servings

◆ Also terrific with Lipton Recipe Secrets Savory Herb with Garlic Soup Mix.

Crispy Garlic Chicken

Pizza Meat Loaf

1 envelope Lipton Recipe Secrets Onion Soup Mix
2 pounds ground beef
1½ cups fresh bread crumbs
2 eggs
1 small green bell pepper, chopped (optional)
¼ cup water
1 cup Ragú® Old World Style® Pasta Sauce
1 cup shredded mozzarella cheese (about 4 ounces)

1. Preheat oven to 350°F. In large bowl, combine all ingredients except ½ cup pasta sauce and ½ cup cheese.

2. In 13×9-inch baking or roasting pan, shape into loaf. Top with remaining ½ cup pasta sauce.

3. Bake uncovered 50 minutes.

4. Sprinkle top with remaining ½ cup cheese. Bake an additional 10 minutes or until done. Let stand 10 minutes before serving. *Makes 8 servings*

◆ Also terrific with Lipton Recipe Secrets Savory Herb with Garlic Soup Mix.

Recipe Tip

When grating cheese, spray your box grater with nonstick cooking spray and place on a sheet of waxed paper. When you finish grating, clean-up is a breeze. Simply discard the waxed paper and rinse the grater clean.

Pizza Meat Loaf

Onion-Baked Pork Chops

1 envelope Lipton Recipe Secrets Golden Onion Soup Mix
⅓ cup plain dry bread crumbs
4 pork chops, 1 inch thick (about 3 pounds)
1 egg, well beaten

1. Preheat oven to 400°F. In small bowl, combine soup mix and bread crumbs. Dip chops in egg, then bread crumb mixture, until evenly coated.

2. In lightly greased 13×9-inch baking or roasting pan, arrange chops.

3. Bake uncovered 20 minutes or until done, turning once.

Makes 4 servings

◆ Also terrific with Lipton Recipe Secrets Onion, Savory Herb with Garlic or Fiesta Herb with Red Pepper Soup Mix.

Sloppy Onion Joes

1½ pounds ground beef
1 envelope Lipton Recipe Secrets Onion Soup Mix
1 cup water
1 cup ketchup
2 tablespoons firmly packed brown sugar

1. In 10-inch skillet, brown ground beef over medium-high heat; drain.

2. Stir in remaining ingredients. Bring to a boil over high heat.

3. Reduce heat to low and simmer uncovered, stirring occasionally, 8 minutes or until mixture thickens. Serve, if desired, on hoagie rolls or hamburger buns.

Makes 6 servings

Onion-Baked Pork Chop

Skillet Chicken in Creamy Garlic Sauce

- **4 boneless, skinless chicken breast halves (about 1¼ pounds)**
- **2 tablespoons margarine**
- **1 large tomato, diced**
- **1 envelope Lipton Recipe Secrets Garlic Mushroom Soup Mix**
- **¾ cup water**
- **¼ cup whipping or heavy cream**

1. Season chicken, if desired, with salt and ground black pepper. In 12-inch skillet, melt margarine over medium-high heat and brown chicken. Remove chicken and set aside.

2. In same skillet, add tomato and cook, stirring occasionally, 2 minutes or until tender. Add soup mix blended with water and cream. Bring to a boil over high heat. Reduce heat to low.

3. Return chicken to skillet and cook 5 minutes or until chicken is no longer pink. Sprinkle, if desired, with grated Parmesan cheese.

Makes 4 servings

Souperior Meat Loaf

1 envelope Lipton Recipe Secrets Onion Soup Mix
2 pounds ground beef
1½ cups fresh bread crumbs
2 eggs
¾ cup water
⅓ cup ketchup

1. Preheat oven to 350°F. In large bowl, combine all ingredients.

2. In 13×9-inch baking or roasting pan, shape into loaf.

3. Bake uncovered 1 hour or until done. Let stand 10 minutes before serving.

Makes 8 servings

◆ Also terrific with Lipton Recipe Secrets Garlic Mushroom, Beefy Onion, Onion-Mushroom, Savory Herb with Garlic or Fiesta Herb with Red Pepper Soup Mix.

Recipe Tip

It's a snap to make fresh bread crumbs. Simply place fresh or day old white, Italian or French bread in a food processor or blender and process until fine crumbs form.

Fast 'n Easy Chili

1½ pounds ground beef
1 envelope Lipton Recipe Secrets Onion Soup Mix
1 can (15 to 19 ounces) red kidney or black beans, drained
1½ cups water
1 can (8 ounces) tomato sauce
4 teaspoons chili powder

1. In 12-inch skillet, brown ground beef over medium-high heat; drain.

2. Stir in remaining ingredients. Bring to a boil over high heat. Reduce heat to low and simmer covered, stirring occasionally, 20 minutes. Serve, if desired, over hot cooked rice. *Makes 6 servings*

First Alarm Chili: Add 5 teaspoons chili powder.

Second Alarm Chili: Add 2 tablespoons chili powder.

Third Alarm Chili: Add chili powder at your own risk.

◆ Also terrific with Lipton Recipe Secrets Beefy Mushroom, Onion-Mushroom, Beefy Onion or Fiesta Herb with Red Pepper Soup Mix.

Fast 'n Easy Chili

Country Beef Pot Pie

- 1 pound ground beef
- 1 bag (16 ounces) frozen mixed vegetables, thawed
- 1 envelope Lipton Recipe Secrets Onion Soup Mix
- 1½ cups milk
- 2 tablespoons grated Parmesan cheese
- 2 tablespoons all-purpose flour
- 1 package (12 ounces) refrigerated biscuits

1. Preheat oven to 375°F. Grease 2½-quart casserole; set aside.

2. In 12-inch skillet, brown ground beef over medium-high heat; drain. Stir in vegetables, soup mix, milk, cheese and flour. Bring to a boil over high heat.

3. Spoon into prepared casserole. Cut biscuits in half and arrange cut side down on hot mixture.

4. Bake 20 minutes or until biscuits are golden. *Makes 4 servings*

Recipe Tip

For the easiest Vegetable Cream Cheese, combine 1 envelope Lipton Recipe Secrets Vegetable Soup Mix, 2 packages (8 ounces each) softened cream cheese and 2 tablespoons milk. Chill at least 2 hours. Serve, if desired, with sliced bagels.

Garlic Mushroom Stir-Fry

2 tablespoons olive or vegetable oil
1 pound boneless, skinless chicken breasts or boneless beef sirloin or pork tenderloin, cut into ¼-inch slices
6 cups assorted fresh vegetables*
1 envelope Lipton Recipe Secrets Garlic Mushroom Soup Mix
1¼ cups water

1. In 12-inch skillet, heat 1 tablespoon oil over medium-high heat and lightly brown chicken. Remove and set aside.

2. In same skillet, heat remaining 1 tablespoon oil and cook assorted fresh vegetables, stirring occasionally, 5 minutes. Stir in soup mix blended with water. Bring to a boil over high heat.

3. Reduce heat to low and simmer uncovered 3 minutes. Return chicken to skillet and cook 1 minute or until chicken is no longer pink. Serve, if desired, over hot cooked rice. *Makes 4 servings*

*Use any combination of the following: broccoli florets, snow peas, thinly sliced red or green bell peppers or thinly sliced carrots.

Recipe Tip

For a quick family pleaser, serve Garlic Mushroom Stir-Fry over couscous instead of rice. Couscous is a tiny-grained semolina pasta that cooks up quickly. Simply add the couscous to boiling water, let stand 5 minutes, fluff and serve.

Lipton RECIPE SECRETS RECIPE SOUP MIX

Chicken & Broccoli with Garlic Sauce

2 tablespoons olive or vegetable oil
4 boneless, skinless chicken breast halves (about 1¼ pounds)
1 package (10 ounces) frozen broccoli florets, thawed
1 envelope Lipton Recipe Secrets Garlic Mushroom Soup Mix
1 cup water
3 tablespoons orange juice
1 teaspoon soy sauce

1. In 12-inch skillet, heat oil over medium-high heat and brown chicken. Remove chicken and set aside.

2. In same skillet, add broccoli and soup mix blended with water, orange juice and soy sauce. Bring to a boil over high heat.

3. Return chicken to skillet. Reduce heat to low and simmer covered 10 minutes or until chicken is no longer pink. Serve, if desired, over hot cooked rice.

Makes 4 servings

Recipe Tip

To quickly thaw frozen broccoli, place in a colander and rinse under warm running water until thawed or microwave at High (full power) 1 minute.

Chicken & Broccoli with Garlic Sauce

Herbed Chicken and Potatoes

- **2 medium all-purpose potatoes, thinly sliced (about 1 pound)**
- **4 bone-in chicken breast halves (about 2 pounds)***
- **1 envelope Lipton Recipe Secrets Savory Herb with Garlic Soup Mix**
- **⅓ cup water**
- **1 tablespoon olive or vegetable oil**

1. Preheat oven to 425°F. In 13×9-inch baking or roasting pan, add potatoes; arrange chicken over potatoes.

2. Pour soup mix blended with water and oil over chicken and potatoes.

3. Bake uncovered 40 minutes or until chicken is no longer pink and potatoes are tender. *Makes 4 servings*

*Substitution: Use 1 (2½- to 3-pound) chicken, cut into serving pieces.

Recipe Tip

For a zippy crumb topping for vegetable, chicken or tuna casseroles, combine Lipton Recipe Secrets Onion Soup Mix with fresh bread crumbs, melted margarine or butter and shredded cheese; broil until golden.

Golden Onion-Baked Chicken

1 envelope Lipton Recipe Secrets Golden Onion Soup Mix
½ cup plain dry bread crumbs
1 (2½- to 3-pound) chicken, cut into serving pieces

1. Preheat oven to 375°F. In medium bowl, combine soup mix with bread crumbs. Moisten chicken with water, then dip in bread crumb mixture, coating well.

2. In large shallow baking pan arrange chicken; drizzle, if desired, with melted margarine or butter.

3. Bake uncovered 45 minutes or until chicken is no longer pink.

Makes 4 servings

◆ Also terrific with Lipton Recipe Secrets Garlic Mushroom, Savory Herb with Garlic or Onion Soup Mix.

Recipe Tip

Chicken should always be cooked until the meat is no longer pink and the juices run clear. The most accurate way to tell if chicken is thoroughly cooked is to check the internal temperature using an instant-read meat thermometer. Insert the thermometer into the thickest part of the chicken without touching the bone. Chicken breasts should reach an internal temperature of 170°F, legs and thighs 180°F.

Chicken Pot Pie

2 cups cut-up cooked chicken
1 package (10 ounces) frozen mixed vegetables, thawed
1¼ cups milk
1 envelope Lipton Recipe Secrets Garlic Mushroom Soup Mix
1 pie crust or pastry for single-crust pie

1. Preheat oven to 400°F. In large bowl, combine chicken and vegetables; set aside.

2. In small saucepan, bring milk and soup mix to a boil over medium heat, stirring occasionally. Cook 1 minute. Stir into chicken mixture.

3. Pour into 9-inch pie plate. Top with pie crust. Press pastry around edge of pie plate to seal; trim excess pastry, then flute edges. With tip of knife, make small slits in pastry.

4. Bake uncovered 35 minutes or until crust is golden.

Makes 4 servings

◆ Also terrific with Lipton Recipe Secrets Herb with Garlic, Golden Onion or Onion Soup Mix.

Chicken Pot Pie

15-Minute Stew

1 tablespoon olive or vegetable oil
1 pound boneless sirloin steak, cut into 1-inch cubes
1 envelope Lipton Recipe Secrets Onion Soup Mix
1 cup water
2 tablespoons tomato paste
1 can (14½ ounces) new potatoes, drained and cut into chunks
1 package (10 ounces) frozen peas and carrots

1. In 12-inch skillet, heat oil over medium-high heat and brown steak.

2. Stir in remaining ingredients. Bring to a boil over high heat.

3. Reduce heat to low and simmer uncovered, stirring occasionally, 10 minutes or until steak is tender.

Makes 4 servings

Garlic Chicken Tenders

2 tablespoons margarine or butter, melted
1 envelope Lipton Recipe Secrets Garlic Mushroom Soup Mix
1½ pounds chicken tenders or boneless, skinless chicken breast halves, cut in strips

1. In small bowl, combine margarine with soup mix. Add chicken to soup mixture and let stand 5 minutes.

2. Heat 10-inch nonstick skillet over medium-high heat 3 minutes or until hot.

3. Add chicken mixture and cook, stirring occasionally, 6 minutes or until chicken is no longer pink. Serve, if desired, with your favorite dipping sauce or on buns with lettuce, tomato, mayonnaise or mustard or in warm flour tortillas with salsa.

Makes 4 servings

Country-Style Chicken Cutlets

- **1 envelope Lipton Recipe Secrets Golden Onion Soup Mix**
- **¾ cup bread crumbs**
- **¼ cup grated Parmesan cheese**
- **1 teaspoon dry mustard (optional)**
- **6 boneless, skinless chicken breast halves, pounded thin, or turkey cutlets (about 1¾ pounds)**
- **1 egg**
- **1 teaspoon water**
- **2 tablespoons margarine or butter, melted**

1. Preheat oven to 350°F. In medium bowl, combine soup mix, bread crumbs, cheese and mustard. Dip chicken in egg beaten with water, then bread crumb mixture until evenly coated.

2. In lightly greased 13×9-inch baking or roasting pan, arrange chicken; drizzle with margarine.

3. Bake uncovered 20 minutes or until chicken is no longer pink, turning once.

Makes 6 servings

◆ Also terrific with Lipton Recipe Secrets Onion, Savory Herb with Garlic or Fiesta Herb with Red Pepper Soup Mix.

Weekend Specialties

Roasted Chicken au Jus

1 envelope Lipton Recipe Secrets Garlic Mushroom Soup Mix
2 tablespoons olive or vegetable oil
1 (2½- to 3-pound) chicken, cut into serving pieces
½ cup hot water

1. Preheat oven to 425°F. In large bowl, combine soup mix and oil; add chicken and toss until evenly coated.

2. In bottom of broiler pan without rack, arrange chicken. Roast chicken, basting occasionally, 40 minutes or until chicken is no longer pink.

3. Remove chicken to serving platter. Add hot water to pan and stir, scraping brown bits from bottom of pan. Serve sauce over chicken.

Makes 4 servings

◆ Also terrific with Lipton Recipe Secrets Savory Herb with Garlic Soup Mix.

Roasted Chicken au Jus

Garlic Mushroom Chicken Melt

4 boneless, skinless chicken breast halves (about 1¼ pounds)
1 envelope Lipton Recipe Secrets Garlic Mushroom Soup Mix
1 can (14 ounces) diced tomatoes, undrained or 1 large tomato, chopped
1 tablespoon olive or vegetable oil
½ cup shredded mozzarella or Monterey Jack cheese (about 2 ounces)

1. Preheat oven to 375°F. In 13×9-inch baking or roasting pan, arrange chicken. Pour soup mix blended with tomato and oil over chicken.

2. Bake uncovered 25 minutes or until chicken is no longer pink.

3. Sprinkle with mozzarella cheese and bake an additional 2 minutes or until cheese is melted.
Makes 4 servings

Barbecued Meat Loaf

1 envelope Lipton Recipe Secrets Onion Soup Mix
2 pounds ground beef
1½ cups fresh bread crumbs
2 eggs
¾ cup water
⅔ cup barbecue sauce

1. Preheat oven to 350°F. In large bowl, combine all ingredients except ⅓ cup barbecue sauce.

2. In 13×9-inch baking or roasting pan, shape into loaf. Top with reserved barbecue sauce.

3. Bake uncovered 1 hour or until done. Let stand 10 minutes before serving.
Makes 8 servings

Garlic Mushroom Chicken Melt

Lipton
RECIPE SECRETS
RECIPE SOUP MIX

Harvest Pot Roast With Sweet Potatoes

- **1 envelope Lipton Recipe Secrets Onion Soup Mix**
- **1½ cups water**
- **¼ cup soy sauce**
- **2 tablespoons firmly packed dark brown sugar**
- **1 teaspoon ground ginger (optional)**
- **1 (3- to 3½-pound) boneless pot roast (rump, chuck or round)**
- **4 large sweet potatoes, peeled, if desired, and cut into large chunks**
- **3 tablespoons water**
- **2 tablespoons all-purpose flour**

1. Preheat oven to 325°F. In Dutch oven or 5-quart heavy ovenproof saucepot, combine soup mix, water, soy sauce, brown sugar and ginger; add roast.

2. Cover and bake 1 hour 45 minutes.

3. Add potatoes and bake covered an additional 45 minutes or until beef and potatoes are tender.

4. Remove roast and potatoes to serving platter and keep warm; reserve juices.

5. In small cup, with wire whisk, blend water and flour. In Dutch oven, add flour mixture to reserved juices. Bring to a boil over high heat. Boil, stirring occasionally, 2 minutes. Serve with roast and potatoes.

Makes 6 servings

Home-Style Beef Brisket

1 envelope Lipton Recipe Secrets Onion Soup Mix
3/4 cup water
1/2 cup ketchup
1 teaspoon garlic powder
1/2 teaspoon ground black pepper
1 (3-pound) boneless brisket of beef

1. Preheat oven to 325°F. In 13×9-inch baking or roasting pan, add soup mix blended with water, ketchup, garlic powder and pepper.

2. Add brisket; turn to coat.

3. Loosely cover with aluminum foil and bake 3 hours or until brisket is tender. If desired, thicken gravy. *Makes 8 servings*

◆ Also terrific with Lipton Recipe Secrets Onion-Mushroom, Beefy Mushroom, Beefy Onion, Savory Herb with Garlic or Fiesta Herb with Red Pepper Soup Mix.

Recipe Tip

For a quick one-dish dinner, add 1/2 pound carrots, cut into 2-inch pieces and 1 pound potatoes, peeled, if desired, and cut into 2-inch chunks during last hour of baking.

Roasted Chicken & Garlic Provençale

1 envelope Lipton Recipe Secrets Garlic Mushroom Soup Mix
3 tablespoons olive oil
2 tablespoons water
1 tablespoon white wine vinegar (optional)
1 (2½- to 3-pound) chicken, cut into serving pieces
1 large onion, cut into 8 wedges
1 large tomato, cut into 8 wedges

1. Preheat oven to 425°F. In small bowl, blend soup mix, oil, water and vinegar.

2. In bottom of broiler pan without rack, arrange chicken, onion and tomato. Evenly pour soup mixture over chicken and vegetables.

3. Roast 45 minutes or until chicken is no longer pink.

Makes 4 servings

Recipe Tip

Recipes prepared in the style of Provence, a region in southeastern France, are typically prepared with garlic, tomatoes and olive oil. Other ingredients common to this region include onions, olives, mushrooms, anchovies and eggplant.

Roasted Chicken & Garlic Provençale

Hearty Beef Stew

4 slices bacon
2 pounds boneless beef chuck or round steak, cut into 1-inch cubes
1 large clove garlic, finely chopped
1 envelope Lipton Recipe Secrets Beefy Mushroom Soup Mix
1 can or bottle (12 ounces) beer or 1½ cups water
1 cup water
1 tablespoon red wine vinegar

1. In Dutch oven or 6-quart saucepot, brown bacon until crisp. Remove bacon, crumble and set aside; reserve 1 tablespoon drippings.

2. Brown beef in two batches in reserved drippings. Remove beef and set aside.

3. Add garlic to drippings and cook over medium heat, stirring frequently, 30 seconds. Return beef to Dutch oven. Add soup mix blended with beer and 1 cup water. Bring to a boil over high heat.

4. Reduce heat to low and simmer covered, stirring occasionally, 1 hour 15 minutes or until beef is tender. Skim fat, if necessary. Stir in vinegar and sprinkle with bacon. *Makes 8 servings*

◆ Also terrific with Lipton Recipe Secrets Onion, Onion-Mushroom, Beefy Onion or Fiesta Herb with Red Pepper Soup Mix.

Chicken Tuscany

- 1 (2½- to 3-pound) chicken, cut into serving pieces
- 1 medium red or green bell pepper, cut into strips
- 1 jar (4½ ounces) sliced mushrooms, drained
- 1 envelope Lipton Recipe Secrets Onion Soup Mix
- 1 can (14½ ounces) whole peeled tomatoes, undrained and chopped
- ½ cup orange juice or water
- 2 tablespoons firmly packed brown sugar
- 1 tablespoons olive or vegetable oil (optional)

1. Preheat oven to 425°F. In 13×9-inch baking pan, arrange chicken, red pepper and mushrooms; set aside.

2. In medium bowl, combine remaining ingredients; pour over chicken.

3. Bake uncovered 50 minutes or until chicken is no longer pink.

Makes 4 servings

Recipe Tip

It's easy to substitute your favorite bone-in chicken parts (all legs, breasts or thighs) for a whole cut-up chicken. Just be sure to substitute the same amount by weight.

Southwestern Meat Loaf

1 envelope Lipton Recipe Secrets Onion Soup Mix
2 pounds ground beef
2 cups (about 3 ounces) cornflakes or bran flakes cereal, crushed
1½ cups frozen or drained canned whole kernel corn
1 small green bell pepper, chopped
2 eggs
¾ cup water
⅓ cup ketchup

1. Preheat oven to 350°F. In large bowl, combine all ingredients.

2. In 13×9-inch baking or roasting pan, shape into loaf.

3. Bake uncovered 1 hour or until done. Let stand 10 minutes before serving. Serve, if desired, with salsa. *Makes 8 servings*

◆ Also terrific with Lipton Recipe Secrets Onion-Mushroom or Beefy Onion Soup Mix.

Recipe Tip

For a great lunchbox treat, wrap leftover meat loaf slices in a tortilla and top with your favorite taco toppings such as salsa, sour cream, grated cheese and shredded lettuce.

Southwestern Meat Loaf

Chicken Smothered in Onions

4 boneless, skinless chicken breast halves (about 1¼ pounds)
2 medium onions, cut into wedges
1 envelope Lipton Recipe Secrets Garlic Mushroom Soup Mix
1 tablespoon firmly packed brown sugar
3 tablespoons margarine or butter, melted
1 tablespoon water

1. Preheat oven to 375°F. In 13×9-inch baking pan, arrange chicken and onions. In small bowl, combine remaining ingredients; pour over chicken.

2. Bake uncovered 30 minutes or until chicken is no longer pink and onions are tender. *Makes 4 servings*

Herb-Crusted Roast Beef

1 envelope Lipton Recipe Secrets Onion Soup Mix
½ cup plain dry bread crumbs
¼ cup margarine or butter, melted
1 tablespoon prepared Dijon-style mustard
1 (3- to 4-pound) top round, rump or eye round roast

1. Preheat oven to 350°F. In small bowl, combine soup mix, bread crumbs, margarine and mustard.

2. In 13×9-inch baking or roasting pan, arrange roast on rack. Press soup mixture onto roast.

3. Bake uncovered 1½ hours or until done. Garnish, if desired, with chopped fresh parsley. *Makes 6 servings*

Savory Chicken Savoy

1 (2½- to 3-pound) chicken, cut into serving pieces
¾ cup balsamic vinegar
1 envelope Lipton Recipe Secrets Savory Herb with Garlic Soup Mix
2 teaspoons dried oregano leaves, crushed
2 tablespoons grated Parmesan cheese

1. Preheat oven to 450°F. In 13×9-inch baking or roasting pan, arrange chicken.

2. In small bowl, combine remaining ingredients; pour over chicken.

3. Bake uncovered, turning and basting once, 45 minutes or until chicken is no longer pink. *Makes 4 servings*

Buffalo Meat Loaf

1 envelope Lipton Recipe Secrets Onion Soup Mix
2 pounds ground beef
1½ cups fresh bread crumbs
½ cup chopped celery
2 eggs
⅓ cup water
⅓ cup Wish-Bone® Blue Cheese Dressing
¼ cup hot pepper sauce

1. Preheat oven to 350°F. In large bowl, combine all ingredients.

2. In 13×9-inch baking or roasting pan, shape into loaf.

3. Bake uncovered 1 hour or until done. Let stand 10 minutes before serving. *Makes 8 servings*

Garlic 'n Lemon Roast Chicken

- **1 small onion, finely chopped**
- **1 envelope Lipton Recipe Secrets Savory Herb with Garlic Soup Mix**
- **2 tablespoons olive or vegetable oil**
- **2 tablespoons lemon juice**
- **1 (3½-pound) roasting chicken**

1. In large plastic bag or bowl, combine onion and soup mix blended with oil and lemon juice; add chicken. Close bag and shake, or toss in bowl, until chicken is evenly coated. Cover and marinate in refrigerator, turning occasionally, 2 hours.

2. Preheat oven to 350°F. Place chicken and marinade in 13×9-inch baking or roasting pan. Arrange chicken, breast side up; discard bag.

3. Bake uncovered, basting occasionally, 1 hour and 20 minutes or until meat thermometer reaches 180°F. (Insert meat thermometer into thickest part of thigh between breast and thigh; make sure tip does not touch bone.)

Makes 4 servings

◆ Also terrific with Lipton Recipe Secrets Fiesta Herb with Red Pepper Soup Mix.

Garlic 'n Lemon Roast Chicken

Hearty BBQ Beef Sandwiches

1 envelope Lipton Recipe Secrets Onion Soup Mix
2 cups water
½ cup chili sauce
¼ cup firmly packed light brown sugar
1 (3-pound) boneless chuck roast
8 kaiser rolls or hamburger buns, toasted

1. Preheat oven to 325°F. In Dutch oven or 5-quart heavy ovenproof saucepot, combine soup mix, water, chili sauce and sugar; add roast.

2. Cover and bake 3 hours or until roast is tender.

3. Remove roast; reserve juices. Bring reserved juices to a boil over high heat. Boil 4 minutes.

4. Meanwhile, with fork, shred roast. Stir roast into reserved juices and simmer, stirring frequently, 1 minute. Serve on rolls. *Makes 8 servings*

Recipe Tip

Always measure brown sugar in a dry measure cup and pack down firmly. To soften hardened brown sugar, place in glass dish with 1 slice of bread. Cover with plastic wrap and microwave at HIGH 30 to 40 seconds. Let stand 30 seconds; stir. Remove bread.

Hearty BBQ Beef Sandwich

Country-Style Pot Roast

1 (3- to 3½-pound) boneless beef pot roast (rump, chuck or round)
1 envelope Lipton Recipe Secrets Onion-Mushroom Soup Mix
2½ cups water
4 medium potatoes, cut into 1-inch chunks (about 2 pounds)
4 carrots, thinly sliced
2 to 4 tablespoons all-purpose flour

1. In Dutch oven or 6-quart saucepot, brown roast over medium-high heat. Add soup mix blended with 2 cups water. Bring to a boil over high heat.

2. Reduce heat to low and simmer covered, turning roast occasionally, 2 hours.

3. Add vegetables and cook an additional 30 minutes or until vegetables and roast are tender; remove roast and vegetables.

4. Blend remaining ½ cup water with flour; stir into Dutch oven. Bring to a boil over high heat. Reduce heat to low and simmer uncovered, stirring constantly, until thickened, about 5 minutes. *Makes 8 servings*

◆ Also terrific with Lipton Recipe Secrets Onion, Beefy Onion, Beefy Mushroom or Fiesta Herb with Red Pepper Soup Mix.

Shredded Garlic Chicken

2 tablespoons olive or vegetable oil
4 boneless, skinless chicken breast halves (about 1¼ pounds)
3 cups frozen Oriental-style vegetables, partially thawed
1 envelope Lipton Recipe Secrets Garlic Mushroom Soup Mix
1 cup water
2 tablespoons soy sauce
1 can (15½ ounces) black beans, drained

1. In 12-inch skillet, heat 1 tablespoon oil over medium-high heat and cook chicken, stirring occasionally, until chicken is no longer pink. Remove chicken and set aside.

2. In same skillet, heat remaining 1 tablespoon oil over medium-high heat and cook vegetables, stirring occasionally, 3 minutes.

3. Meanwhile, with fork, shred chicken. Return chicken to skillet. Stir in soup mix blended with water and soy sauce. Bring to a boil over high heat. Stir in beans and cook, stirring occasionally, 2 minutes or until heated through.

Makes 4 servings

Recipe Tip

Shredded Garlic Chicken is terrific served as is, but for an easy hand held meal try wrapping it in tortillas. Warm flour tortillas for a few minutes in your oven, on your grill or over a gas flame. Or wrap each tortilla in a damp paper towel and microwave at High (full power) 10 seconds. Fill with shredded chicken mixture. Enjoy!

Lipton RECIPE SECRETS RECIPE SOUP MIX

Can't Get Enough Chicken Wings

18 chicken wings (about 3 pounds)
1 envelope Lipton Recipe Secrets Savory Herb with Garlic Soup Mix
½ cup water
2 to 3 teaspoons hot pepper sauce* (optional)
2 tablespoons margarine or butter

1. Cut tips off chicken wings (save tips for soup). Cut chicken wings in half at joint. Deep fry, bake or broil until golden brown and crunchy.

2. Meanwhile, in small saucepan, combine soup mix, water and hot pepper sauce. Cook over low heat, stirring occasionally, 2 minutes or until thickened. Remove from heat and stir in margarine.

3. In large bowl, toss cooked chicken wings with hot soup mixture until evenly coated. Serve, if desired, over greens with cut-up celery.

Makes 36 appetizers

*Use more or less hot pepper sauce as desired.

Recipe Tip

The tips from the chicken wings can be used to make your own chicken stock. Simmer wing tips with water, onion, celery, bay leaf and any other vegetables or herbs you desire for 1 to 2 hours. Strain stock and skim off the fat. Freeze in containers or self-closing plastic bags for later use.

Index